GLEE CLUB™

MUSIC PERFORMANCE

VOCALS AND BAND

CHRISTINE KOHLER

ROSEN
PUBLISHING®

NEW YORK

Deep gratitude to my dad, Dwight Rhodeback, and band director, Charles Temple, for teaching me discipline and an appreciation for music

Published in 2013 by The Rosen Publishing Group, Inc.
29 East 21st Street, New York, NY 10010

Library of Congress Cataloging-in-Publication Data

Kohler, Christine, 1953–
Music performance: vocals and band/Christine Kohler. — 1st ed.
    p. cm. — (Glee club)
Includes bibliographical references and index.
ISBN 978-1-4488-6875-9 (library binding) — ISBN 978-1-4488-6885-8 (pbk.) —
ISBN 978-1-4488-6886-5 (6-pack)
1. Glee clubs. I. Title.
MT930.K64 2013
782.5 — dc23

                                                                    2011048499

Manufactured in the United States of America

CPSIA Compliance Information: Batch #S12YA: For further information, contact Rosen Publishing, New York, New York, at 1-800-237-9932.

CONTENTS

INTRODUCTION

Suddenly it's cool again to take singing out of the shower and into the glee club. Thanks to TV hits like *Glee*, even geeks can be singing gleeks and jocks are strutting their stuff onstage. If your school doesn't have a glee club, why not be the one to step onto center stage and start one?

Everything has to start somewhere. In the United States, glee clubs began in March 1853 at Harvard University in Massachusetts. During the nineteenth century, the all-male Harvard Glee Club sang musical arrangements ranging from old European and American college and folk songs to contemporary art songs to popular operetta and show tunes. The singers were accompanied by banjo and mandolin ensembles and local bands.

Glee clubs, also known as show choirs, which combine choral singing and synchronized dance routines, burst on the

In Season 1 of the television show *Glee*, (*front left to right*) Amber Riley and Chris Colfer perform "The Power of Madonna." *Glee* led to a revival of glee clubs in many U.S. high schools.

scene in the mid-1960s in the Midwest. In 1974, seven show choirs attended the first competition in Fort Wayne, Indiana.

Before FOX aired *Glee* in the fall of 2009, there were about two hundred glee clubs in U.S. schools. Within a year, that number swelled to about six hundred. This phenomenon was dubbed the "*Glee* effect."

There are a lot of great reasons to start a glee club. Maybe you find you can't stop tapping your foot and humming along to music. Simply enjoying music and singing is a good reason to start a glee club. Also, glee clubs are a great place to socialize with other people who love music and want to learn and perform different types of music, from classical to jazz, show tunes to pop and rock.

Maybe you want to improve your vocal skills. You may have a voice for chorus, but with some professional training you might be chosen for solos.

There is a reason why some people sing only in the shower. Singing in front of a crowd can be nerve-wracking. But performing in front of an audience can help the singer overcome anxiety and build self-confidence.

Being in a glee club can also give you an idea of whether you would like to pursue a music career or even give you the skills and experience to enjoy a lifelong hobby singing. Careers in music come in different packages—choir directors in schools or community and church choirs, to actors or directors on Broadway. Maybe you dream of becoming a singing sensation, cutting albums and touring. All professional musicians had to start somewhere. Why not you? And why not start by singing and performing in a glee club?

Glee club today, stardom tomorrow!

CHAPTER 1

STARTING A GLEE CLUB

Don't warm up your vocal cords just yet. The first step in forming a club—any club—is to find out the rules at the place you want to support your group. Most glee clubs are school-sponsored. If your school does have a choir, talk to the choir director about what it would take to start a glee club. Perhaps you need to take the issue up with the principal, superintendent, or school board—whoever has the power to make the decision. Read the handbook and know the rules for clubs at your school.

Who will be responsible for the club and who will direct? The choir director is the best choice because he or she is an expert in vocal training. A second choice for a glee club would

The choir director might be the biggest advocate and supporter of a school glee club. He has the necessary training to organize and run a successful glee club or show choir.

be a drama teacher experienced in directing musicals. If it is an after-school club not under the umbrella of the choir director or drama teacher, then find another faculty member who has experience in vocals to be the club sponsor.

If your school does not have a show choir and you want to start one, then prepare a proposal. The person with the authority to make the decision, such as the principal or superintendent, will pay more attention to a well-prepared proposal that demonstrates how a glee club will benefit students. Here are some facts and information to include in the proposal to prove that gleeks are no slackers.

Proposal Showing Educational Value of Glee

Students who join a chorus have higher self-confidence, self esteem, self-discipline, and increased memory skills, and they are better problem-solvers, according to a 2009 research poll commissioned by Chorus America. These facts ought to impress the administrator with the power to approve a glee club.

Scott C. Shuler, president of the National Association for Music Education (MENC), said at MENC.org that statistics prove "schools that have strong music programs report higher graduation rates and fewer dropouts than those that don't."

In addition, most colleges recommend one or two years of music for admission, according to a U.S. Department of Education handbook.

Those are just a few strong arguments to point out in a proposal in favor of why your school should support a glee club.

Give Options for Practice Schedules

Overcome objections before they can be raised when asking for permission to start a glee club. One question that arises is the matter of when and where to hold practices. A myriad of activities vie for space and time at school.

If glee club is part of the choir program, then maybe class schedules can be arranged so that choir members have the same homeroom and block schedules, with choir scheduled as a core subject, rather than as extracurricular. Glee club then becomes a breakout group from the overall choir, just as jazz band is made up of members from the concert and marching bands.

However, this scheduling is sometimes difficult if students are on different tracks—college, business, vocational—and may exclude some students from being able to work choir and glee club into their schedules.

Another option is to hold glee club practice after school two to three times a week. Be flexible, though. If the administrator says that many times interfere with the use of facilities for other groups, it may be that glee club practices will have to be only once a week after school. Still, negotiate for increased rehearsals during times closer to performances.

Request to practice in the place where performances will be held, such as the school auditorium or gymnasium. It is better to work in a place where the acoustics will be most like where the glee club will perform. That way, there are no surprises in sound changes and space to move about on opening night. Again, if this is not possible, be willing to compromise. Nevertheless, ask to use the performance room during rehearsals for several weeks before opening night.

Money Makes a Difference

Cost is a big issue. Many programs in the arts either don't exist or have been axed because of budget cuts at some level of the educational system. Glee clubs can be quite expensive because of the cost of sound equipment, music, costumes, and travel. Some clubs even hire professional choreographers and sound engineers. To introduce a proposal to add glee club, you have to prove how the program can be funded.

Ask someone in administration how much of school funds are designated for non-core curriculum activities. Do a little research and find out how much money and support, if any, groups such as journalism, yearbook, band, athletics, and other clubs get from the school budget. This will give you an idea about how much can be reasonably expected to ask for in regard to financial support from the school. Keep in mind, though, that if your school does not already have a choir, adding a glee club will be competing for funds designated for those other activities. This means the other activities would be expected to receive fewer funds. That's why the issue of starting a choir, and glee club, may have to be taken up with the school board.

Parents can be your biggest supporters. Just like football boosters and band boosters, your parents can form a glee booster club. The boosters can organize large-scale fundraisers. They can also solicit private businesses for donations of money, goods, and services.

Grants, Fund-raisers, and Paid Performances

Some schools have a grant writer on staff, or the superintendent applies for grants. But grant writing is speculative. Grants take a lot of time to research and write, and the competition is very stiff. Still, it's not impossible to get a grant. Start by looking at choral and music organizations' Web sites and check for grants. Download all the rules and forms. Ask the principal if someone at the school would do the paperwork to apply for the grant. If this is not possible, ask if any glee or choir parents have experience in grant writing and would be willing to apply for the grant.

No matter how much money activities receive from the school, parents, or sponsoring businesses, club members will

Put the fun in fund-raisers! Even washing cars can build teamwork that can spill over to working together effectively in a show choir.

still have personal expenses, such as uniforms and trips. Glee club members can do fund-raisers: bake sales, car washes, selling wrapping paper or pizza, or running booths at fairs, to name just a few. Select fund-raisers that will raise the largest amount of money and are practical products people might buy anyway.

Once the glee club has had some training, and lots of practice, then it is possible to get invitations to sing and perform. Some places pay; others will give donations to the glee club.

SOME FACTS ON CHOIR

Choir members aren't quitters. A 2006 Harris Poll found 90.2 percent graduate rates in schools with music programs compared to 72.9 percent graduation rates at schools without music programs.

Choir teaches self-discipline and gives students an incentive to show up for school. Schools with music programs have higher attendance rates at 93.3 percent compared to 84.9 percent attendance rates at schools without music programs, according to a 2006 Harris Poll.

Presenting the Proposal

Once you have the proposal prepared, make an appointment with whoever is the decision-maker. This is a business meeting, so present your proposal in a calm, nonemotional manner and with a positive attitude. Administrators will be impressed that you've done your homework and have come to the meeting with facts and solutions.

If for some reason the school administrator decides against your proposal to have a glee club, don't give up. As they say in show business, "The show must go on!" Look around the community for other possibilities.

Maybe there is a community arts center or theater group that would work with your youth show choir. For example, in the San Francisco Bay area in California there are about forty children's vocal ensembles, all independent of public schools. Many of

The San Francisco Boys Chorus and the San Francisco Girls Chorus sing in Washington, D.C., on January 20, 2009, before the swearing-in ceremony for President Barack Obama.

these groups are world-class talent, including the San Francisco Girls Chorus and San Francisco Boys Chorus, which both performed at President Barack Obama's inauguration in 2009.

Recruiting Singers

Now that you've prepared a winning proposal and persevered to find a sponsor, it's time to recruit musicians.

The most likely source of talent that has already had some vocal training is in the choir. If the choir director is not the glee sponsor, then ask the director to make an announcement

Band members often play in marching, concert, and jazz bands, so they are adept at performing a variety of music. Some musicians even play more than one instrument.

about tryouts during choir practice. Besides school choirs, many people sing in church choirs. And don't forget the shy shower singers. Maybe they are just waiting to be asked to join an organized glee club. So make announcements during homeroom and post in prominent places, such as the halls and cafeteria, snazzy posters and a sign-up sheet with the time, date, and place of the first organizational meeting.

Tap into the band for two areas, instrumental and vocals. If glee club practice doesn't interfere with scheduled band practices, extend the invitation to band members. Don't assume because they play instruments that they can't also sing. Band members usually begin playing their instruments by fifth grade and have a rigorous music education that includes sight-reading, music theory and composition, and music appreciation.

Marching band members are accustomed to learning choreographed routines, memorizing music, playing by ear, playing harmony, keeping a beat, staying in tune, and transposing to different keys. They already have the musical training; find out if they can also sing.

Now that you have recruited singers, Maestro, strike up the music!

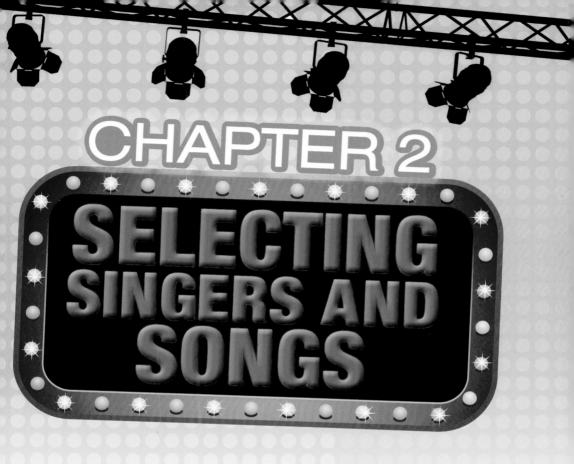

CHAPTER 2

SELECTING SINGERS AND SONGS

You have hit a high note by gaining approval for a glee club. Pick up the tempo; it's time to select singers and music.

Before tryouts, decide if the glee club will be open to everyone, regardless of ability. Many people can learn to sing well enough to blend into a chorus. But not everyone will be a soloist. Keep in mind that singing voices don't fully mature until people are in their twenties. That's one way in which the TV and movie high school musicals are deceptive; older actors often play younger characters.

J. Prentice Loftin, director of the El Paso Conservatory of Music in Texas, says when recruiting singers for glee club, he looks for "good pitch, wide range, beauty of sound, strong parental support, well-focused and disciplined" singers.

The exceptional few singers who belt out full, rich tones in their preadolescent years on shows such as *American Idol* are rare. In adolescence, boys especially have trouble with their voices cracking. So during tryouts, don't expect everyone to sound as good as professionals. Expect untrained musicians who are eager to learn.

Besides singing abilities, have those trying out for the choral group answer a questionnaire to determine any previous experience in music.

If it's a show choir, add a short and simple choreographed dance routine to tryouts. It will give those assessing abilities a chance to see if the student has a sense of rhythm and can pick up routines easily. However, if it comes down to selecting a fabulous dancer who can't sing and a singer who is an awkward dancer, go with the latter. In other words, put the emphasis on "choir" over "show." Most people can be taught to dance, but many people will never develop good singing voices.

Music Genres

Whoever selects the music may pick tunes from genres you aren't necessarily familiar with, like classical or big band. Or the director may decide to have the show choir perform a mix of foreign songs and dances.

Classical music was written during the late eighteenth and nineteenth centuries in Europe. Some glee clubs, especially at universities, sing primarily classical music. During the pilot episode of *Glee*, the Swingle Singers performed "Moonlight Sonata" by Ludwig van Beethoven and "Flight of the Bumblebee" by Nikolai Rimsky-Korsakov.

All That Jazz and Show Tunes

Big band music is an ensemble of musicians who play jazz music of the "Swing Era" of the 1930s and 1940s. Many of the Swing Era hits were primarily instrumental. Instruments typically used in the band were saxophones, trumpets, trombones, guitar, piano, string bass, and a drum. But vocalists also played a big part in the big band era. Some of the biggest hits of the Swing Era were the Andrew Sisters' "Boogie Woogie Bugle Boy," Bing Crosby's "I'm Dreaming of a White Christmas," and Nat King Cole's "It's Only a Paper Moon." Many famous big band songs even made the leap onto the big screen, prominently featured in popular movies of the day.

Jazz originated in the twentieth century in New Orleans and combined elements of European-American and African music. It is an often-improvised, expressive style of music, characterized by syncopated rhythms, notes in a blues style, and use of the seventh and ninth chords. "When the Saints Go Marchin' In" is an example of jazz with vocals. Ella Fitzgerald is considered the "First Lady of Song" of the Jazz Age. She sang such hits as "Night and Day" and had a range that spanned three octaves.

The Andrew Sisters' career spanned from the 1930s through the 1990s. In the 1940s, (*clockwise from back left*) Patty, LaVerne, and Maxene also starred in at least seventeen films.

Broadway musicals, which include show tunes, are written for performance on the theater stage. Musicals, developed in the twentieth century in America and England, are similar to European operettas, which contain spoken dialogue, unlike operas. Musicals tend to feature songs that are comparable to popular songs of the day, ensembles, and dance. This is why musicals are ideal for performance by show choirs—they are written with the intent of choreographed dance to accompany the songs.

Disco, Pop, and Rock

In one of the early episodes of *Glee,* the choir director wanted the glee club to perform a disco song. The cast groaned, and the lead singer rebelled and replaced the disco song with a contemporary song. Disco may not be popular in the twenty-first century, but in the 1970s people who wanted to dance went to a club called a discotheque. This is where the term "disco" came from, to describe dance music.

Karen Lynn Gorney (as Stephanie) and John Travolta (as Tony) exemplified disco dancing under the glittery disco ball in the 1977 film *Saturday Night Fever.*

"I Will Survive," first sung by Gloria Gaynor in 1978, was considered the anthem of disco, although it didn't have the dubbing and remix of other disco hits. For a quick immersion in disco style, watch *Saturday Night Fever*, a movie starring John Travolta as dance king of the club.

Rock music, also called rock 'n' roll, began in the 1950s in the United States, but it swiftly became popular with teens throughout the world. In the late 1960s and 1970s, many British rock composers and performers, such as the Beatles, became famous in the United States, then achieved worldwide fame. Rock music is characterized by a driving backbeat, electric guitar, and vocals.

Selecting Background Music

Part of the decision as to whether or not to have background music to accompany the glee club will depend upon the

A CHORAL DIRECTOR ON THE *GLEE* PHENOMENON

"I watch the show [*Glee*]…to see what kinds of arrangements they're doing and what artists they're representing. And then my students come in and say, 'I heard this great song,' or 'I heard this great arrangement,' on *Glee*. So I think they're doing a great service in showing a variety of musical styles, eras and genres, and demonstrating how pieces can be crossed from one style to another." —Choral director Daniel Gregerman of Niles North High School in Skokie, Illinois, in an interview with Christopher Loudon in *Jazzy Times*.

strength of the voices. One difficulty for untrained or preteen and teen voices is lack of projection in tone and volume.

Some glee clubs sing *a cappella*, which means they sing without any instrumental music. One advantage is that the background music won't drown out the vocals.

Even if the glee club sings *a cappella*, a piano should be used in the practice room. It provides accompaniment and tonal and rhythmic assistance while preparing new songs. The piano also helps you hear the music as you read the notes on sheet music.

Selecting Music Based on Availability and Cost

You may be singing the latest releases from contemporary recording artists along with a favorite radio station or iPod download, but that doesn't mean any song is available to sing for glee club or show choir performances.

There are a lot of considerations for what songs to select. Beyond considering the vocal range of the glee club members, you must also weigh the cost of obtaining the music. It would be nice if you could just download from iTunes any song you fancy, but it doesn't work that way—at least not legally—because songs are copyrighted. The recording artists need to get paid, and that happens through royalties on each copy sold.

Copyrights protect the printing and duplication of music. The director must purchase as many copies of sheet music

PAUL MCCARTNEY: *GLEE* FAN

Former Beatle Paul McCartney is a fan of *Glee* and has sent a mix tape wish list of what songs of his that he would like performed on the show. Not all contemporary bands are fans of *Glee*, though. Damon Albarn, the front man for Blur and Gorillaz, and rock band Kings of Leon refuse to let the show cover their songs.

Paul McCartney, formerly with the Beatles (1960–1970) and Wings (1971–1981), is a British musician and composer listed in the Guinness World Records as the most successful musician and composer in popular music history.

as will be used in rehearsal. Some directors file the originals and distribute photocopies. All duplicated copies should be destroyed when no longer needed. Prices vary based on the style, length, and publishing house. When purchasing sheet music, performance rights information is often noted in the product description.

Many songs on the radio are either not released as sheet music or there are no choral arrangements available from the publishers. There is usually a lag between when songs make the charts and when a choral arrangement has been composed and published.

All choral music not in public domain has copyright and performance restrictions. Most of these rights are obtained by contacting the music publisher, since most composers sell the rights to the publisher.

The performance rights of music may be waived if the musical piece is performed only in the classroom, for a nonprofit performance, or where funds are used for educational or charitable purposes.

Picking Music for Best Performance

Besides the cost of permission rights, another consideration when selecting music is the available talent in your particular glee club. Most middle school and high school singers don't have the maturity of sound like college students and singers in their twenties and older, so choose music that will showcase their abilities instead of music that demands choral techniques for more mature voices. It can hurt a singer's individual singing style long-term.

You also don't want to pick music based on the spectacular voice of one person. It's considered unethical, and, besides, what if he or she drops out of glee club? Your whole program will go down the tubes and the director will have to start over, with less time to prepare the next selection.

So, whatever music your director chooses, have a spirit of adventure and learn the tune and words with a positive attitude.

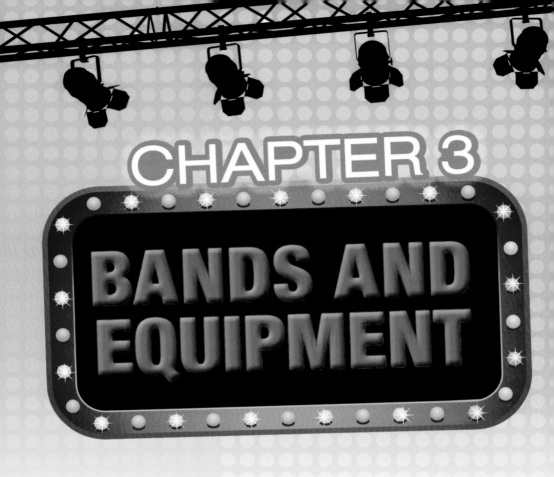

CHAPTER 3
BANDS AND EQUIPMENT

If your glee club decides not to sing *a cappella*, then these options will need to be weighed for background music.

There are advantages to using a piano during performances. A skilled pianist doesn't drown out the singers. A piano also takes away the need for a baton-waving conductor, which can distract from the performers.

Using a piano eliminates separate rehearsals for and with a band. Often, it is difficult to switch to singing with a band in dress rehearsal after using a piano only during practices.

Live bands can be ideal, provided the instruments, especially drums, don't overpower the singers' voices. Acrylic drum shields can overcome this problem. Pianos are essential for vocal practices.

Also, pianos can sound monotonous during performances. The richness of color of band music can be lost.

CD background music is recommended for each singer to take home and use for practicing. However, "canned" CD background music is inflexible during practice. If singers and dancers mess up, a pianist can start again or smooth over the flub and get the performers back on track. But the CD just keeps spinning, leaving performers on their own to recover from mistakes.

For competitions, though, most glee clubs use show choir tracks because the orchestrations are fuller and enhance the overall impact of the music, according to Kyle Cannons, artistic director for California Artist's Academy.

Band Rules

So, if all these pros and cons have left your glee club deciding on an instrumental band, look at using a small ensemble. No, it doesn't have to be like the banjo and mandolin ensembles that accompanied the original Harvard Glee Club. Instead, consider a small ensemble with the type of instruments used in a jazz band—clarinets, saxophones, piano, guitars, and percussion. Whatever instruments make up the band, the sound needs to be subdued.

Backup musicians need to harmonize and be able to play pianissimo—that means very softly. The singers are the stars in a show choir, so instrumentals should keep the volume low.

Live music with a choir can be great, but it can also have its limitations. The number of instruments in the band depends on the size and vocal skill of the choir, as well as the style and type of performance. If you have a strong instrumental program at the school, and the genre of music aligns with the musicians available, then live music is definitely an option.

When auditioning band members, see if they can play in a manner considerate of the singers. After all, a glee club should showcase the vocals; the band should only be background music to enhance the singers.

Equipment

Equipment will be the biggest expense with running a glee club. This is another advantage to having a glee club under the umbrella of the choir director, who already has access to resources such as a piano and electronic equipment and practice rooms. But let's go over the equipment you may need for a successful glee club in case your sponsorship comes from other sources.

Purchasing Sheet Music

Singers need sheet music, which can be purchased at a music store, through publisher representatives, or online. Music stores buy single copies of many songs, from classics to the latest releases. Many music stores have headphones and electronic equipment for the buyer to listen to the songs while visiting the store. Often, music store owners make up "conductor packets," which the choir director can purchase with a limited return policy. This gives the director a chance to study the music and

REASONS TO GET INVOLVED IN MUSIC

Musicians tend to be smart and successful later in life. Many go to college and choose higher-paying careers. A 2008 Harris study commissioned by the National Association for Music Education (MENC) found people who were involved in music tend to become better educated and earn more than those who weren't involved in music programs.

try it out for a short time before deciding whether to commit to purchasing sheets for the entire choir.

Each singer needs his or her own sheet music with individual parts for soprano to bass, plus the entire score for the director and student conductor, if your group has one. The band also requires its own sheet music; each member needs the score for that particular instrument.

If you check out music online, even if you don't buy it online, there are usually audio links.

Podiums, CD Players, Video Recorders, and DVD Players

Many conductors require a portable podium or a step stool so that they can be seen by the entire group. Check the hardware store for a stool-toolbox combination. This will make a handy place to store the sheet music and baton and small supplies, especially when the group is traveling.

A CD player that also records is a must. Video recorders and DVD players can also be helpful for glee clubs. That way, you can watch yourselves after rehearsals to look for mistakes or places for improvement, like how coaches and sports teams watch play-by-play videos after a game. Some choir directors videotape their show choirs once they are performing well and post the videos on YouTube.

Sound Systems

Ideally, you want to find a place to perform that has natural acoustics because microphones tend to distort the sound. In smaller venues, or with certain styles of music such as *a cappella* and classical, or where the size and skill of the ensemble does not need amplification, microphones may not be necessary.

There is nothing worse than the audience not being able to hear those four-part harmonies, after several months of rehearsals. A sound system, microphones, and speaker amplification system are sometimes necessary for performances if the room acoustics are poor.

Glee clubs use microphones in a variety of ways, depending on the venue. They use wide-range microphones for ensemble work, with or without wireless body pack mics for soloists in large venues. Just make sure, in advance, that the competitions you plan to enter allow sound equipment.

For performances that use choreography, think about investing in small body pack wireless microphones. Good-quality body pack microphones are expensive, especially because one is needed for each member of the club. Get recommendations on high-quality equipment for the best price from someone in the music recording business before purchasing. It would be irritating to find out the microphone gives bad feedback or screeches with static when the volume is turned up, or that it doesn't pick up all the voice tones.

The twenty-first century is a digital high-tech age with new technology popping up every year, so consider finding someone locally who can be trusted as a knowledgeable and experienced sound engineer. Sound engineers and sound-boards can be worth the cost.

Instruments

A piano will be your most expensive investment, if the school doesn't already own one. It should be in the practice room. And although it might be tempting to look at more high-tech equipment, like electric keyboards and synthesizers, they cannot replace the sound quality of a piano. Some music instructors use all three—if the budget allows.

Uniforms

It is usual for glee club members to wear uniform clothes or costumes. Often, a very formal look is preferred, such as black velvet and satin or taffeta dresses for girls, and black tie and cummerbund suits for guys, or even snazzier showman costumes in bright-colored satin and sequins.

Glee clubs can require a variety of costumes, depending on the theme and style of program presented. Props may even be necessary to go along with the choreography.

Some glee club groups wear simple, yet elegant, black dresses for girls and white shirts and black slacks for boys. For a more formal style, the guys may also wear black bow ties and cummerbunds.

Before making a decision about what the glee club should wear as a group, you may want to consider your budget first. Then allow glee club members to vote on their costume preferences. Should you order your costumes from a catalog or have them made? These are all things to be considered.

Rehearsal Location

Schools hire professionals to design the choir rooms, practice rooms, and auditoriums. Larger rooms with vibrant acoustics will likely be where the glee club performs. Sometimes, glee clubs will not be able to rehearse in the same room where they will perform. If this is the case, make sure you can at least practice

FAMOUS GLEE CLUB MEMBERS

What do the following famous people all have in common: Ashton Kutcher, Pink, Barbra Streisand, Sheryl Crow, Cole Porter, and three U.S. presidents—Woodrow Wilson, Theodore Roosevelt, and Franklin D. Roosevelt? They all performed in glee clubs while in high school or college. In fact, while Porter sang in the Yale Glee Club, he also composed more than three hundred songs!

in the performance room a number of times before the program. Acoustics can change everything concerning the sound.

Some choir rooms have risers. This may depend upon the size of the glee club.

Outside venues present challenges that might not be able to be overcome unless the place is already wired with microphones. Otherwise, the sound can get lost in the wind or crowds.

Transportation

Even professional groups own tour buses and have to pay for gasoline and repairs. Lucky for you, most schools have provisions for school buses to be used for after-school functions involving school clubs. But there still might be a fee. Check with your sponsor or principal about the cost of transportation.

Once you've decided on background music and have obtained equipment, location, and transportation, the real work begins. *Mi, mi, mi, mi-i-i-i*…It's time to sing!

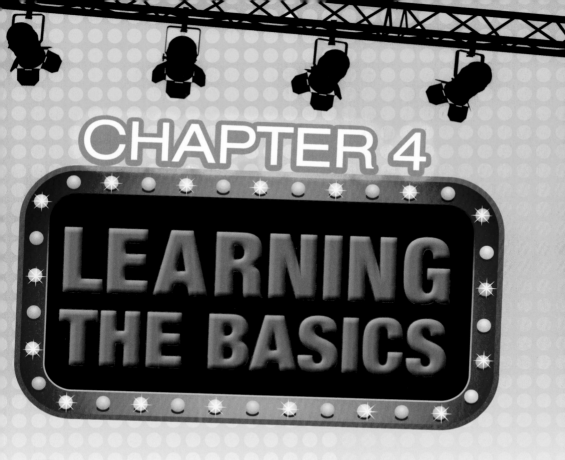

CHAPTER 4

LEARNING THE BASICS

Do, re, mi, fa, so, la, ti, do...Doe a deer, a female deer. Ray, a drop of golden sun. Me a name, I call myself. Fa, a long long way to run...

If you are thinking, "I've got a long way to run up and down these scales before I perform, and even longer until I hit the big time," you are right. There is more to singing than just opening your mouth and belting out some words. Singers must learn techniques, such as how to breathe from their diaphragms, properly open the mouth and throat as if holding an egg in it so as not to pinch the sound, listen to and match tones, do voice

Singing with a choir takes practice, not only learning to hit the notes in the right key but also listening to other parts and harmonizing so that all parts blend in one rich melody.

builders to increase range, and harmonize. Be patient with the process. Be patient with yourself. Relax and have fun!

It is also beneficial to learn how to read music. This way, you can sight-read music you've never seen or heard before. Some schools require students involved in musical programs to take music theory tests. If the musician decides to create original compositions, he or she will need to know how to read and write music.

Private Practice Options

Like in sports, in order to improve, you must practice, practice, practice singing. But the old adage "Practice makes perfect" is not true if mistakes aren't corrected during practice.

"Practice not for hours, but for results," according to Archie Jones in *Music Education in Action: Basic Principles and Practical Methods.*

Private lessons are especially important when first starting out. A private tutor can point out weak spots in your singing technique that may go unnoticed when you are blending in with the group. You can also improve at the pace right for you.

During group tryouts for parts, the leader is concerned with getting the best voice. The emphasis has to be on what is best for the whole group. But in private lessons, all that matters is improving your skills so that for future tryouts, you have a chance to stand out and, hopefully, get picked for the choice parts.

That's an advantage of private lessons with a voice teacher or coach. One drawback of private lessons is that they can be costly. Talk to your choir director. Someone may be willing to coach you for free or for a low rate. If not, ask him or her for recommendations outside of school. Also look around the community for theater groups or community choirs. These sources for private lessons may be more flexible in scheduling than the school choir director. Check with a church to see if anyone in the choir has a music degree with an emphasis on vocals. You may find a music minister, or maybe a pastor's spouse with a music degree, open to supplementing his or her income by giving private lessons.

Another place to check is at a music store, or ask music professors at local colleges. If the professors are too busy or charge too much, ask for a recommendation of an accomplished college student-musician at the university or music

Private lessons give a singer the one-on-one attention she needs to improve weak areas and excel among stiff competition. Make the most of private lessons by practicing on your own between sessions.

conservatory. College students who are music majors may be less expensive and eager to gain experience working with students.

Practice on Your Own, with Mentor

With or without private lessons, schedule a time daily to practice on your own. Don't strain the vocal cords by practicing too long at one time. Perhaps the glee club can start a mentor program where more accomplished singers partner with novices and practice together once a week. The more experienced singer could help the beginner singer with learning to read music and hear pitches and notes. The mentor would benefit because, as teachers know, one learns by instructing others. It would also bond the group together. When more accomplished singers mentor, they may feel less frustrated and powerless to improve the overall quality of the entire glee club.

Sectional and Group Practices with Student Leaders

As scheduling permits, only the sopranos, altos, tenors, or basses practice together in sectional practices. These sectional practices may take place before school or during a common period, such as library hour or study hall, depending upon what time works best for everyone in your section.

FUN DANCING FACTS

- Tap dancing originates from Irish clog dancing, called the Irish reel and jig.
- The world's largest disco, comprised of thirteen thousand people, danced at the Buffalo Convention Centre, New York, in 1979, according to the *Guinness Book of World Records*.
- In August 1983, Peter Stewart of Birmingham, United Kingdom, set a world record by disco dancing for 408 hours.
- The father of hip-hop dance, Clive Campbell, came to New York from Jamaica in 1967. Hip-hop derived from a Caribbean music called reggae. Break dancing was born out of hip-hop.

Most vocal practices will include the entire glee group.

Sometimes, though, subsections can be broken out of the whole group to practice on individual parts and a small area of the music that needs to be learned or perfected. In this case, a sectional practice with student leaders can be overseen by one adult director.

Student section leaders chosen by the director may lead sectional practice. Section leaders may not necessarily be the best singers in the choir. They are more likely older, more experienced students of good character who show themselves to be responsible leaders. They also need to know the keys on the piano so that they can hit the right notes for pitch.

Student vocalist mentors, section leaders, and chore-ographers may train to become student directors. Student directors do some conducting and choreography, help orga-nize rehearsal schedules, and delegate responsibilities.

Learning Dances

Vocal practice and dance practice should be conducted sepa-rately until both are to a level where they can be combined.

When introducing new choreography, go over the steps slowly and break them down into sections. Next, combine the steps with background music. This is where CDs for everyone to take home are helpful. Also, consider pairing students who catch on to dance steps quickly with students who have more difficulty picking up the dance moves. Maybe students could be matched with practice partners who live near them so that

FUN MUSIC FACTS

- The compact disc (CD) was developed by Philips and Sony in 1980.
- A DVD disc is the same diameter and thickness as a CD, but a DVD can store thirteen times more data.
- Forty billion songs are downloaded illegally per year; that's 90 percent of all music downloads.
- Global sales of prerecorded music total more than $40 billion.

they can get together evenings and weekends outside of formal practices.

One of the most common errors is to always start a choral or dance rehearsal on the first song of the planned program. The beginning of the performance will likely be well learned, while the rest of the numbers may suffer. Instead, start with the numbers you feel need the most work.

If using a live band for accompaniment, don't wait until dress rehearsal to bring in the band to the practice.

Summer Practice

Unlike other school subjects, musicians don't put away their music at the end of a school term, never to listen or sing again until the next school year begins. Singing or playing an instrument becomes ingrained into the fabric of a musician's

Small group practice sessions can meet in relaxed informal settings. Besides the benefits of practicing an instrument or singing, small group sessions are a great way to develop friendships with other musicians.

daily life. Since vocalists sing during the summer, too, why not continue the formal training as well?

You may want to consider attending a summer camp dedicated to music. There are camps for band members and vocalists, and even glee camps. Check online for camps that fall within your budget.

Are you on a tight budget or just don't want to spend too much of your summer away from home? Check into weekly summer voice classes. Without the pressure of academic credits, or preparing for a performance, the atmosphere may be more relaxed.

Warm-up Tips

Before you ever go to practice or rehearsal, there are things you can do to make the most of your session. It is important to warm up your vocal cords before rehearsal. If not, you can damage your voice.

Don't let the sectional practice last too long. Shorter sessions with more frequent practices can yield more lasting results. Take practice sessions seriously. Don't skip out for other events. Go to practice with a dedication and commitment to the group. You'll get out of it what you put into it. Practice with a purpose. Imagine the end result and how exciting it will be to hear the applause after a stellar performance.

CHAPTER 5

PERFORMANCES

Now that your glee club is organized, trained, singing harmoniously, and dancing rhythmically, it's showtime!

Choirs, bands, and orchestras put on at least two concerts a year, usually one in December and one in the spring. Sometimes, the glee club is part of the combined concert, or it schedules a separate show. These concerts are usually held in the evening and are open to the general public.

Besides concerts, the glee club or individual singers can perform at sporting events. The glee club or soloists could sing the "Star-Spangled Banner" or school alma mater before some athletic games.

You, too, could be on YouTube! Many glee club and show choir directors show off the talent of their gifted singers by posting stellar performances on YouTube for, literally, the whole world to see.

Perhaps the band director would be open to allowing the glee clubs to perform a song and dance number at a football halftime show.

You may also want to consider posting videos of performances online. YouTube opens up a public forum with an international audience. Just be sure your glee club is performing at a level that will make you all proud to be seen on YouTube!

Community Performances

Look to the community for opportunities to perform, too. A community theater may welcome a performance from the glee club. Some other venues to explore for performing experience would be rodeos, charity events, fairs, and theme parks.

Like the school marching band, the glee club could march and sing in community parades. Just be sure to wear comfortable shoes because some of those parade routes can be long or uphill. If the marching groups stop in front of a reviewing stand of spectators, this is a chance to show off a short song and dance number. These events are often televised. The school band director would be the best one to ask for information on parade invitations.

Activities directors at nursing homes, senior centers, adult day care centers, and hospitals often welcome singers to entertain residents and clients. Many senior citizens love to have children and teens visit because the communities are often limited to an older generation. They love seeing the energy and zest of children and teens. Visiting and singing is a great way to help brighten their lives.

Competitions

When choosing competitions to attend, select reputable ones. Don't have too high expectations in the beginning. Competitions are expensive due to travel, hotels, and registration fees. So, look first at local and state competitions to gain experience and see how your glee club compares to others in your region.

"Go where you will be stretched, but also be affirmed," says Kyle Cannons, artistic director of California Artist's Academy.

A fifth-grade glee club from P.S. 22, the largest elementary school in New York City, sings at the 2009 National Christmas Tree Lighting ceremony at the White House.

If your glee club wins national competitions, then it will move into the elite league of glee clubs that compete in international competitions. In 2011, the San Francisco Girls Chorus became the first American vocal ensemble to win a place in the finals of Let the Peoples Sing, a choral competition organized by the European Broadcasting Union.

Then there are the dream invitations—for instance, when the San Francisco Girls Chorus and the San Francisco Boys Chorus performed at President Obama's inauguration in 2009. Or when the San Francisco Boys Chorus and the Robert Moses' Kin dance company performed in a multimedia "Fable and Faith" production in February 2011 at the Yerba Buena Center for the Arts in California. Or when the Ragazzi Boys Chorus from California toured Cuba in the summer of 2011. Or when the fifth-grade glee club at P.S. 22 of Graniteville, Staten Island, New York, sung at the National Christmas Tree Lighting ceremony at the White House in December 2009 and the 74th Academy Awards in 2011. Their choir director also blogs about them and posts videos of their performances on YouTube.

Tips for a Winning Performance

Yes, it is important to select quality music, a compatible dance routine, and complementary accompaniment. It is imperative to have practiced and harmonized your voices properly. Costumes and props add pizzazz and professionalism.

Yet, uniformity is the key element to putting on a stellar show, according to Dr. Jason Heald, chairman of the Fine and Performing Arts Department at Umpqua Community College in Oregon. As a composer, performer, educator, and director of choral groups that perform and compete, Dr. Heald gave the following tips in the *Oregon Choral Focus* for a winning performance.

COOL KIDS JOIN CHOIR

Glee club and choir members are not necessarily the misfits shown on *Glee*. Singers in schools actually have a lot of company. According to the Chorus Impact Study commissioned in 2009 by Chorus America, more than ten million children and teens participate in school choirs in the United States.

Uniformity in Appearance

Concert choirs have a long tradition of performance attire, such as robes and tuxedos, which provides a unified look for the ensemble. Attire for a contemporary ensemble can run from formal wear to T-shirts and jeans.

The most critical aspect of dress is to avoid wearing anything that draws attention to an individual. If a group is wearing matching short-sleeved T-shirts and one member wears a long-sleeved shirt under the T-shirt, this will be distracting. But if everyone wears a long-sleeved undershirt, then uniformity is

Although several males in the back row are wearing black shirts and the girls have different colored scarves, no one is dressed in a distracting fashion. Even the sheet music is bound in simple black folders.

kept. Other distracting items include excessive or large jewelry, big belts, brightly colored shoes, or hats. You want the audience or judges to concentrate on your voices, not your accessories.

Uniformity in Actions

Glee clubs are often encouraged to "move with the music" to avoid a stiff performance. But this can result in a contrived appearance, overactive singers, and even bizarre performance behavior. A more effective approach, according to Heald, is to relax and be naturally affected by the music. To help you relax, stand up straight, yet slightly flex your knees and elbows. When singing as a group, performers should avoid any behavior or gestures that attract individual attention. In theatrical terms, this is referred to as "pulling focus." Strong gestures such as pointing, making faces, and miming the music are distracting.

However, if a performer is featured as a soloist, then he or she should step forward with authority and feel free to make any gestures that enhance the message of the music. The soloist is the focus and must have a commanding presence. The group should be more reserved when a soloist is in the forefront to avoid distracting audience members.

Choreography, by definition, should provide uniformity in behavior. However, attention to detail becomes even more critical because any variation in movement between individuals can be very apparent to the audience. Every gesture must be executed with crisp exactness by everyone in the group or the result may be slipshod or amateurish.

Connecting with the Audience

Eye contact is one of the most valuable tools you have to connect with the audience. Traditional choirs always have a focal point—the conductor. As a result, they appear focused and engaged, and this energy is transferred to the audience. But if your glee club has no conductor, the group's focus can be diffused and pull audience attention away from the music.

Members should work at making direct eye contact with the audience. If the focus is too low, such as staring at the floor, the performer will look sleepy. If the focus is too high, such as staring at the ceiling, the performer will look disengaged. Instead, your gaze should be steady and straight-ahead. Also avoid shifting your eyes from side to side. Focus on a point in the audience on which to concentrate your gaze.

And finally, add a healthy dose of self-confidence to your abilities. Smile!

Keep on Believin'

You may not receive fabulous invitations to perform at the White House or Academy Awards. Your glee club may not even win competitions. But the important thing is to follow your passion, sing your heart out, and enjoy the journey, whether or not it leads to stardom. Now "Take a Bow" and "Keep on Believin'"!

GLOSSARY

a cappella Singing without instrumental music.

acoustics The qualities of a room that have to do with how clearly sounds can be heard in it.

amplification The act of making something louder.

backbeat The downbeat in a rhythm.

chords Any combination of notes simultaneously performed.

choreographer The person who designs the movement of a dance.

composition The "putting together" of notes to make a melody or harmony, or adding words to the music.

copyright The legal right to have control over the work of a writer, artist, or musician. The owner of the copyright of the intellectual property must be paid by other people to broadcast, publish, or perform it.

diaphragm A sheet of muscle that separates the thoracic cavity from the abdominal cavity.

dubbing Adding sound to a tape.

harmony Musical notes that accompany the melody, which is the main musical strand of a song. It is often described as the clothing of the melody.

music theory The study of the theoretical elements of music, including sound and pitch, rhythm, melody, harmony, and notation.

octaves The series of eight degrees between a tone and any of its octaves.

public domain A book, play, or music with intellectual rights that have expired or been forfeited; it can be used by anyone and is not protected by copyright.

syncopation A displacement of the beat or the normal accent of a piece of music.

synthesizer An electronic machine that produces and combines different sounds, especially for music.

FOR MORE INFORMATION

American Choir Directors Association
545 Couch Drive
Oklahoma City, OK 73102-2207
(405) 232-8161
Web site: http://acda.org/repertoire
The American Choir Directors Association provides support for
directors of choirs at all levels. The Web site posts information,
including a video of an award-winning show choir and radio
links to classical choral music.

Association of Canadian Choral Communities
A-1422 Bayview Avenue
Toronto, ON M4G 3A7
Canada
(416) 927-7291
Web site: http://choralcanada.org/ACCC_en
The Association of Canadian Choral Communities supports choir
conductors, choirs, and administrators, including participation in
choral festivals and competitions in Canada and internationally.
Check out the student conductor internship for Canadian
musicians.

Canadian Music Educators Association
Box 849
Terrance Bay, ON P0T 2W0
Canada
Web site: http://www.cmea.ca
The Canadian Music Educators Association offers $200 grants
to provinces to hold conferences. It also sponsors song-
writing competitions for all ages, amateurs, and published
composers.

Chorus America
1156 15th Street NW, Suite 310
Washington, DC 20005
(202) 331-7577
Web site: http://www.chorusamerica.org
Chorus America is an organization, based in the nation's capital, that provides directors with information, research, leadership development, and professional training, including a conducting master class.

Music Educators National Conference (MENC)
1806 Robert Fulton Drive
Reston, VA 20191
(703) 860-4000
(800) 336-3768
Web site: http://www.menc.org
The Music Educators National Conference advocates for music education and gives facts, quotes, research, and statistics on music education.

NAMM Foundation: International Music Products Association
5790 Armada Drive
Carlsbad, CA 92008
(760) 438-8001 ext. 102
Web site: http://www.nammfoundation.org/music-research
NAMM offers more than half a million dollars in grants and scholarships. There is an essay contest for students twelve and under. It is also a clearinghouse for donating and receiving instruments for schools.

National Endowment for the Arts
1100 Pennsylvania Avenue NW
Washington, DC 20506-0001

(202) 682-5400
Web site: http://www.nea.gov/grants/apply/index.html
The National Endowment for the Arts posts government grants for
    the arts.

National High School Musical Theatre Awards
1450 Broadway, 6th Floor
New York, NY 10018
(412) 281-3973
Web site: http://www.nhsmta.com
The National High School Musical Theatre Awards recognizes
    individual artistry in vocal, dance, and acting performance.
    Judges select a best actor and actress from high school musicals
    who win a chance to participate in a study program with a
    professional theater in New York City.

New York State School Music Association
718 The Plain Road
Westbury, NY 11590-5931
(516) 997-7200
Web site: http://nyssma.org
The New York State School Music Association awards student com-
    posers and gives them an opportunity to attend a composition
    coaching workshop and young composer seminars. (Check your
    region for similar competitions and awards.) There is also infor-
    mation on how qualifying schools can apply for $50,000
    scholarships from a $1 million donation from the TV show *Glee*.

Texas Music Educators Association
7900 Centre Park Drive
Austin, TX 78754
(888) 318-8632

(512) 452-0710
Web site: http://www.tmea.org
The Texas Music Educators Association offers grant applications for
    grants totaling $1 million, available to Texas public schools for
    programs in dance, music, theater, and art.

Web Sites

Due to the changing nature of Internet links, Rosen Publishing
has developed an online list of Web sites related to the subject
of this book. This site is updated regularly. Please use this link
to access the list:

http://www.rosenlinks.com/glee/band

FOR FURTHER READING

Angel, Ann. *Janis Joplin: Rise Up Singing*. New York, NY: Amulet Books, 2010.

Balser, Erin, and Suzanne Gardner. *Don't Stop Believin': The Unofficial Guide to Glee*. Toronto, ON, Canada: ECW Press, 2010.

Freeman, Hilary. *Loving Danny*. London, UK: Piccadilly Press, 2006.

Gervay, Susanne. *That's Why I Wrote This Song*. Sydney, Australia: HarperCollins Australia, 2007.

Great Musicians. New York, NY: DK Eyewitness Books, 2008.

Jeffrey, Gary, and Terry Riley. *Bob Marley: The Life of a Musical Legend*. New York, NY: Rosen Publishing, 2006.

Klickstein, Gerald. *The Musician's Way: A Guide to Practice, Performance and Wellness*. New York, NY: Oxford University Press, 2009.

Lowell, Sophia. *Glee: Foreign Exchange*. New York, NY: Poppy, 2011.

Mack, Valerie Lippoldt. *Putting the Show in Choir: The Ultimate Handbook for Your Rehearsal and Performance*. Nashville, TN: Shawnee Press, 2011.

Nathan, Amy. *Meet the Musicians: From Prodigies (or Not) and Pros*. New York, NY: Henry Holt, 2006.

Nathan, Amy. *The Young Musician's Survival Guide: Tips from Teens & Pros*. 2nd ed. New York, NY: Oxford University Press, 2008.

Peckham, Anne. *The Contemporary Singer: Elements of Vocal Technique*. 2nd ed. Boston, MA: Berklee Press, 2011.

Rickman, Amy. *Gleeful!: A Totally Unofficial Guide to the Hit TV Series Glee*. New York, NY: Villard, 2010.

Ruggles, Lucy. *Camp Rock*. New York, NY: Disney Press, 2008.

Seelig, Timothy. *The Perfect Rehearsal*. New York, NY: Music Sales America, 2006.

Sofras, Pamela Anderson. *Dance Compositions Basics: Capturing the Choreographer's Craft*. Champaign, IL: Human Kinetics, 2006.

Stone, Tanya Lee. *Up Close: Ella Fitzgerald*. New York, NY: Viking Children's Books, 2008.

Wasserman, Robin, Sue Rose, and Laura McCreary. *Unfabulous: Keepin' It Real!* London, UK: Simon & Schuster UK, 2008.

Weaver, Mike, and Colleen Hart. *Sweat, Tears, and Jazz Hands: The Official History of Show Choir from Vaudeville to Glee*. Milwaukee, WI: Hal Leonard, 2011.

Wilson, Leah. *Filled with Glee: The Unauthorized Glee Companion*. Dallas, TX: Smart Pop, 2010.

Wynne-Jones, Tim. *The Uninvited*. Cambridge, MA: Candlewick, 2010.

BIBLIOGRAPHY

AOL News. "Real-Life Glee Club, Chorus from Staten Island, to Sing at Oscars." February 18, 2011. Retrieved July 16, 2011 (http://www.aolnews.com/2011/02/18/real-life-glee-club-chorus-from-staten-island-to-sing-at-oscar).

Benner, Charles. *Teaching Performing Groups*. Washington, DC: Music Educators National Conference, 1972.

Cannons, Kyle. Interview with author. September 2011.

Chen, Stephanie. "The 'Glee' Effect: Singing Is Cool Again." CNN.com, November 15, 2010. Retrieved July 1, 2011 (http://www.cnn.com/2010/LIVING/11/15/glee.effect.show.choir.comeback/?hpt=C2).

Conway, Colleen, and Thomas Hodgman. *Teaching Music in Higher Education*. New York, NY: Oxford University Press, 2009.

Dwyer, Terence. *Opera in Your School*. New York, NY: Oxford University Press, 1964.

Freer, Patrick. *Getting Started with Middle School Chorus*. 2nd ed. Lanham, MD: Rowman & Littlefield Education, 2009.

Heald, Jason. Interview with author. September 2011.

Heald, Jason. "Presentation Is Everything." *Oregon Choral Focus*, May 2011.

Healey, Jeanette, and Ian McCormack. *Getting the Buggers in Tune*. New York, NY: Continuum International Publishing Group, 2008.

Jipson, Wayne. *The High School Vocal Music Program*. West Nyack, NY: Parker Publishing Company, 1972.

Jones, Archie, Ed. *Music Education in Action: Basic Principles and Practical Methods*. Dubuque, IA: WM. C. Brown Company Publishers, 1964.

Kerachsky, Stuart. "National Assessment of Educational Progress. Arts 2008: Music and Visual Arts." National Center for Education Statistics, June 15, 2009. Retrieved July 1, 2011 (http://nces.ed.gov/whatsnew/commissioner/remarks2009/6_15_2009.asp).

Kreger, Bernard. "History of the Harvard Glee Club." Harvard Glee Club. Retrieved September 2011 (http://www.harvardgleeclub.org/info/history).

Lamble, Walter. "The Extracurricular Program: So You Are Going to Do a Musical." *A Handbook for Beginning Choral Educators.* Bloomington, IN: Indiana University Press, 2004.

Loftin, J. Prentice. Interview with author. August 2011.

Loudon, Christopher. "The Glee Effect." *Jazz Times*, September 16, 2010. Retrieved July 1, 2011 (http://jazztimes.com/articles/26514-the-glee-effect).

Rizga, Kristina. "Can Glee Club Reduce High School Dropout Rates?" *Mother Jones*, December 23, 2010. Retrieved July 1, 2011 (http://motherjones.com/media/2010/12/mission-high-choir?page=1).

Sur, William, and Charles Schuller. *Music Education for Teen-agers.* New York, NY: Harper & Row, 1966.

Weidensee, Victor. *Instrumental Music in the Public School.* Boston, MA: Crescendo Publishing Company, 1969.

INDEX

About the Author

Christine Kohler played the cornet starting in fifth grade and performed in the concert, marching, and dance band in high school in Ohio. Kohler now specializes in writing for children and teens, teaches writing, and edits from her home in west Texas.

Photo Credits

Cover (singer) stryjek/Shutterstock.com, (guitarist) Kiselev Andrey Valerevich/Shutterstock.com, (violinist) © istockphoto.com/Cagri Oner, (trumpeter) istockphoto.com/Jacom Stephens; cover, back cover, interior graphics (stars, lit frame) © istockphoto.com/Yap Siew Hoong; back cover, interior graphics (stage lights silhouette) Collina/Shutterstock.com; p. 5 Michael Yarish/© Fox Television/Courtesy: Everett Collection; p. 8 Jetta Productions/Lifesize/Thinkstock; p. 12 Yellow Dog Production/The Image Bank/Getty Images; pp. 14, 47 © AP Images; p. 15 Comstock/Thinkstock; p. 20 Michael Ochs Archives/Getty Images; p. 21 Michael Ochs Archives/Moviepix/Getty Images; p. 24 Rob Verhorst/Redferns/Getty Images; p. 27 © istockphoto.com/Christopher Futcher; p. 28 Mat Hayward/Shutterstock.com; p. 33 © istockphoto.com/Matt Abbe; p. 36 © Jeff Greenberg/PhotoEdit; p. 38 Lisa F. Young/Shutterstock.com; p. 42 © Dennis MacDonald/PhotoEdit; p. 45 © istockphoto.com/Trevor Smith; p. 49 muzsy/Shutterstock.com.

Designer: Nicole Russo; Editor: Bethany Bryan;
Photo Research: Karen Huang